EMMANUEL JOSEPH

From Academia to the Workforce: A Comprehensive Guide for Graduating Students

Copyright © 2023 by Emmanuel Joseph

All rights reserved. No part of this publication may be reproduced, stored or transmitted in any form or by any means, electronic, mechanical, photocopying, recording, scanning, or otherwise without written permission from the publisher. It is illegal to copy this book, post it to a website, or distribute it by any other means without permission.

First edition

*This book was professionally typeset on Reedsy.
Find out more at reedsy.com*

Contents

1 Entering the Labor Market During Your Last Year in College...   1
2 Chapter 2: Self-Assessment   4
3 Chapter 3: Resume Building   8
4 Chapter 4: Networking   12
5 Chapter 5: Internships and Part-Time Jobs   15
6 Chapter 6: Job Search Strategies   19
7 Chapter 7: Interview Preparation   23
8 Chapter 8: Professional Development   27
9 Chapter 9: Career Counseling   31
10 Chapter 10: Building a Personal Brand   35
11 Chapter 11: Transitioning from Academia to the Workforce   39
12 Chapter 12: Thriving in Your New Career   43

1

Entering the Labor Market During Your Last Year in College or University

As a student in your final year of college or university, you stand at the cusp of an exciting and transformative journey—transitioning from the world of academia to the dynamic and ever-evolving labor market. This chapter serves as an introduction to the critical process of preparing for this transition, setting the stage for the chapters that follow.

The Significance of Your Last Year

Your last year in college or university marks a crucial period in your life. It's a time when you'll be wrapping up your academic journey and venturing into the professional world. Understanding the significance of this year is the first step in ensuring that you make the most of it.

1. Bridge to Your Future: The final year acts as a bridge that connects your educational experiences to your future career. It's a unique phase that demands reflection, planning, and action.

2. Preparation is Key: Preparing for the transition to the labor market during this year can significantly impact your future success. The choices you make

now can shape your career trajectory.

3. Competitive Landscape: In an increasingly competitive job market, preparation and proactivity become essential. Employers seek candidates who are not only academically qualified but also well-prepared to excel in the professional world.

The Scope of This Guide

Throughout this guide, we will delve into a comprehensive set of strategies, tools, and resources to empower you in your transition from student to working professional. You will find practical advice, real-world examples, and actionable steps to assist you in navigating the complexities of the labor market during your final year in college or university.

Here's a glimpse of what you can expect in the following chapters:

- Self-Assessment: Understanding your skills, interests, and values to shape your career goals.
  - Resume Building: Crafting a compelling resume that showcases your academic and extracurricular achievements.
  - Networking: Building a professional network and leveraging university resources to create valuable connections.
  - Internships and Part-Time Jobs: Gaining practical experience before graduation to enhance your employability.
  - Job Search Strategies: Effective techniques for finding job opportunities, including online job boards and career fairs.
  - Interview Preparation: Tips for excelling in job interviews, including common questions and strategies.
  - Professional Development: Strengthening your soft skills and attending workshops and seminars to become a well-rounded professional.
  - Career Counseling: Seeking guidance from career advisors to tailor your career path.

- Building a Personal Brand: Managing your online presence and showcasing your expertise.
- Job Offers and Negotiation: Evaluating job offers and negotiating compensation and benefits.
- Making the Transition: Successfully transitioning from college to the workforce and adapting to the demands of the labor market.

As you progress through this guide, you'll gain valuable insights and develop the skills needed to confidently navigate your last year in college or university and make a successful leap into the labor market. Remember, this is a transformative period in your life, and the decisions you make now will shape your future. Let's embark on this journey together and ensure that you're well-prepared to thrive in your future career.

2

Chapter 2: Self-Assessment

Before you can effectively enter the labor market during your last year in college or university, it's essential to have a deep understanding of yourself. This chapter focuses on the critical process of self-assessment, which involves identifying your skills, interests, and values. These insights will help you define your career goals and make informed decisions as you prepare for the professional world.

The Importance of Self-Assessment

Self-assessment is not just a one-time exercise; it's an ongoing process that evolves as you learn and grow. Here's why it's so crucial:

1. Clarifying Your Path: Understanding your strengths and weaknesses, interests, and values provides clarity about your career path. It's the foundation upon which you'll build your professional journey.

2. Goal Setting: Armed with self-assessment insights, you can set specific, achievable career goals. This helps you focus your efforts and make meaningful choices.

3. Personal Growth: Self-assessment isn't just about career planning; it's a

tool for personal growth. It allows you to continuously improve and adapt as you progress in your career.

Identifying Your Skills

1. Academic Skills: Begin by evaluating your academic strengths. What subjects or areas do you excel in? What skills have you honed through your coursework?

2. Soft Skills: Assess your soft skills, such as communication, teamwork, problem-solving, and leadership abilities. These skills are often just as important as technical skills in the job market.

3. Technical Skills: If you have specific technical skills related to your field of study, highlight them. These can be strong selling points on your resume.

Exploring Your Interests

1. Passions and Hobbies: Consider what you are genuinely passionate about. Hobbies and interests can often be translated into fulfilling career choices.

2. Curiosity: What topics, industries, or issues pique your curiosity? Identifying areas of interest can guide your career exploration.

3. Extracurricular Activities: Reflect on your involvement in extracurricular activities. What clubs, organizations, or volunteer work have you found most engaging?

Defining Your Values

1. Core Values: Think about your core values. What principles and beliefs are important to you in a work environment? Is work-life balance a priority, or are you more focused on innovation and creativity?

2. Work Environment: Consider the type of work environment that aligns with your values. Do you prefer a corporate setting, a startup, or perhaps a non-profit organization?

3. Impact: Assess the impact you want to have through your work. Do you aim to make a difference in people's lives, work on cutting-edge technologies, or contribute to a specific cause?

Career Goals

Based on the self-assessment, start setting specific career goals. These goals should be:

1. S.M.A.R.T.: Specific, Measurable, Achievable, Relevant, and Time-bound.

2. Short-Term and Long-Term: Include both short-term goals you can achieve in the near future and long-term objectives that guide your overall career direction.

3. Flexible: Be open to adjusting your goals as you gain more experience and knowledge.

Putting Self-Assessment into Action

- Once you've identified your skills, interests, values, and goals, you can start tailoring your resume, networking, and job search to align with these findings.
    - Seek guidance from career counselors, professors, and mentors to refine your self-assessment and validate your career goals.
    - Continuously revisit and update your self-assessment as you gain new experiences and insights.

Self-assessment is a foundational step in your journey to the labor market. It empowers you to make informed career decisions, ultimately increasing your chances of finding a fulfilling and successful career path. As you move forward in your final year, use these insights to guide your choices and prepare for the opportunities that lie ahead.

3

Chapter 3: Resume Building

Your resume is your first opportunity to make a positive impression on potential employers. This chapter focuses on crafting a professional and tailored resume that effectively showcases your academic and extracurricular achievements, making you stand out in the competitive job market.

The Significance of Your Resume

1. First Impressions: Your resume is often the first document that potential employers see. It's a crucial tool for making a positive first impression.

2. Showcasing Your Skills: A well-structured resume highlights your skills, experience, and qualifications, giving employers a glimpse of what you can bring to the table.

3. Tailored for Success: Tailoring your resume to each job application increases your chances of being selected for an interview. It shows that you've done your homework and are genuinely interested in the position.

Resume Components

CHAPTER 3: RESUME BUILDING

1. Contact Information: Include your name, phone number, email address, and LinkedIn profile (if applicable). Ensure your contact information is up to date.

2. Objective or Summary: A concise statement summarizing your career goals and what you can offer to the employer. Make this section specific to the job you're applying for.

3. Education: List your educational institutions, degree(s) earned, major, graduation date, and relevant academic achievements (e.g., honors, GPA).

4. Relevant Coursework: If you're a recent graduate, consider listing relevant coursework that showcases your knowledge and skills.

5. Work Experience: Include internships, part-time jobs, or any work-related experiences. Describe your responsibilities, achievements, and skills acquired in each role.

6. Extracurricular Activities: Highlight leadership roles or significant contributions in clubs, organizations, or volunteer work. Emphasize relevant skills developed.

7. Skills: Create a skills section to highlight both technical skills (e.g., programming languages) and soft skills (e.g., communication, teamwork).

8. Awards and Achievements: Mention any academic or extracurricular awards or honors you've received.

9. Publications or Projects: If you've published research or completed noteworthy projects, provide details to showcase your expertise.

Tips for Crafting Your Resume

1. Be Concise: Keep your resume concise, ideally one page for recent graduates. Use bullet points and avoid lengthy paragraphs.

2. Customize for Each Job: Tailor your resume for each job application. Highlight skills and experiences that are most relevant to the position.

3. Use Action Verbs: Start each bullet point with a strong action verb to describe your achievements (e.g., "developed," "managed," "implemented").

4. Quantify Achievements: Whenever possible, use numbers to quantify your accomplishments (e.g., "increased sales by 20%").

5. Highlight Transferable Skills: Emphasize skills that can transfer to a variety of roles, such as problem-solving, leadership, and communication.

6. Proofread: Thoroughly proofread your resume to eliminate errors. Consider having someone else review it as well.

7. Professional Formatting: Use a clean and professional format with consistent fonts and headings. Ensure that your resume is easy to read.

Examples and Templates

Consider seeking examples and templates to help you structure your resume effectively. Your university's career center or online resources can provide valuable guidance.

Remember that your resume is a dynamic document that should evolve as you gain more experiences and achievements. Regularly update it to reflect your growth and adapt it to your evolving career goals.

A well-crafted resume is a powerful tool in your job search arsenal. It's your opportunity to demonstrate your qualifications and make a compelling

CHAPTER 3: RESUME BUILDING

case for why you're the ideal candidate for the job. Invest time and effort into creating a standout resume, and you'll be well on your way to securing interviews and landing your desired position.

4

Chapter 4: Networking

Building a strong professional network during your final year in college or university is a valuable asset as you prepare to enter the labor market. This chapter explores the importance of networking, how to cultivate meaningful connections, and how to leverage university resources and alumni networks.

Understanding the Value of Networking

1. Access to Opportunities: Networking provides access to job opportunities, internships, and information that may not be publicly available.

2. Career Guidance: Through networking, you can gain insights and advice from professionals who have already navigated the transition from academia to the workforce.

3. Personal Branding: Building relationships with peers and professionals in your field helps establish your reputation and credibility.

Networking within Your University

1. Attend Career Fairs: Universities often host career fairs where you can

meet with recruiters and learn about job opportunities. These events are excellent opportunities to network.

2. Join Student Organizations: Many universities have student clubs and organizations related to specific fields or interests. Joining these groups can connect you with like-minded peers and potential mentors.

3. Engage with Professors: Professors can be valuable contacts for job recommendations and career advice. Don't hesitate to seek guidance from them.

Leveraging Alumni Networks

1. Alumni Associations: Most universities have alumni associations or networks. Connect with alumni through these associations to access their experience and insights.

2. LinkedIn: LinkedIn is a powerful platform for networking with alumni. Join your university's alumni group and reach out to former students working in your desired field.

Effective Networking Strategies

1. Be Proactive: Initiate conversations and actively seek opportunities to meet new people. Attend events, seminars, and conferences related to your field.

2. Develop a 30-Second Pitch: Craft a concise pitch that introduces yourself, your skills, and your career goals. This is useful for making a memorable first impression.

3. Listen and Learn: When networking, focus on learning from others. Ask questions and show genuine interest in their experiences.

4. Follow Up: After meeting someone, send a follow-up email expressing your appreciation for the conversation and interest in staying connected.

Building Genuine Relationships

1. Authenticity: Be yourself when networking. Authenticity is key to building meaningful connections.

2. Offer Value: Networking is a two-way street. Offer your skills, knowledge, or assistance when you can. Helping others can strengthen your relationships.

3. Diversify Your Network: Connect with people from various backgrounds and industries. A diverse network can offer unique insights and opportunities.

Maintaining Your Network

1. Regular Contact: Stay in touch with your network through occasional emails, messages, or coffee meetings. Don't wait until you need something to reach out.

2. Celebrate Achievements: Share your successes with your network and celebrate their accomplishments. Acknowledging milestones strengthens your connections.

3. Seek Mentorship: Identify potential mentors within your network who can provide guidance as you enter the labor market.

Networking is a continuous process that can have a profound impact on your career journey. Start building your network during your last year in college or university, and nurture it as you transition into the workforce. Your network can be a source of support, mentorship, and opportunities throughout your professional life.

5

Chapter 5: Internships and Part-Time Jobs

Gaining practical experience through internships and part-time jobs is a crucial step in your transition from college or university to the labor market. This chapter explores the benefits of such experiences and offers guidance on how to secure and make the most of them.

The Importance of Practical Experience

1. Real-World Application: Internships and part-time jobs provide the opportunity to apply academic knowledge to practical situations.

2. Skill Development: These experiences help you develop job-specific skills, adaptability, and a better understanding of the professional world.

3. Networking: Internships and part-time positions often introduce you to professionals in your field, expanding your network.

Finding the Right Internship or Part-Time Job

1. Start Early: Begin your search well in advance. Many organizations have application deadlines several months before the position starts.

2. Utilize University Resources: Your career services center can be a valuable resource for finding internship and job opportunities. They may have partnerships with local companies.

3. Online Job Boards: Platforms like LinkedIn, Indeed, and specialized industry job boards can help you identify positions that match your interests and skills.

Crafting an Impressive Application

1. Resume Tailoring: Customize your resume and cover letter for each application. Highlight relevant skills and experiences.

2. Show Enthusiasm: In your cover letter and during interviews, demonstrate your genuine interest in the company and the role.

3. Prepare for Interviews: Be ready to discuss your skills, goals, and how you can contribute to the organization. Research the company to show your knowledge.

Maximizing Your Internship or Part-Time Job

1. Set Clear Objectives: Identify specific goals you want to achieve during your internship or part-time job. Discuss these with your supervisor.

2. Seek Mentorship: Develop relationships with colleagues and supervisors. Ask for guidance and feedback to enhance your learning experience.

3. Take Initiative: Don't wait for tasks to be assigned. Be proactive, volunteer for projects, and demonstrate your willingness to learn and contribute.

Learning from the Experience

CHAPTER 5: INTERNSHIPS AND PART-TIME JOBS

1. Reflect Regularly: Throughout your internship or part-time job, reflect on what you've learned, your accomplishments, and how it aligns with your career goals.

2. Build a Portfolio: Collect evidence of your work, such as reports, projects, and positive feedback, to create a portfolio showcasing your abilities.

3. Network Actively: Connect with colleagues and professionals in the organization. Attend company events and seek informational interviews.

Making a Smooth Transition

1. Express Your Interest: If you hope to secure a full-time position with the organization, express your desire and ask about future opportunities.

2. Collect References: Request letters of recommendation or contact information from supervisors or colleagues who can vouch for your abilities.

3. Evaluate Your Experience: Assess how the internship or part-time job aligns with your career goals. Use this feedback to adjust your career strategy.

Balancing Academics and Work

1. Time Management: Efficiently manage your time to balance academic commitments and work responsibilities.

2. Communication: Keep your professors and employers informed of your academic and work schedules to ensure a smooth balance.

Internships and part-time jobs offer a bridge between the academic world and the labor market. They can provide invaluable experience, enhance your resume, and help you build a network of professional connections. By being proactive, enthusiastic, and reflective, you can make the most of these opportunities as you prepare for your transition into the professional world.

6

Chapter 6: Job Search Strategies

Searching for job opportunities during your last year in college or university can be a daunting task, but with effective strategies, you can navigate the process successfully. This chapter covers various approaches and techniques to find the right job for you.

Diverse Job Search Strategies

1. Online Job Boards: Use websites and platforms like LinkedIn, Indeed, Glassdoor, and specialized industry job boards to search for job openings. Set up job alerts to stay updated on new postings.

2. Company Websites: Visit the career pages of companies you're interested in. Many organizations list their job openings on their websites.

3. Networking: Leverage your professional network, which includes professors, peers, mentors, and alumni, to learn about hidden job opportunities.

4. Career Fairs: Attend job fairs organized by your university or in your area. These events allow you to meet recruiters and learn about job prospects.

5. Recruitment Agencies: Consider working with recruitment agencies or

headhunters who specialize in your field. They can help match you with suitable positions.

6. Cold Outreach: Sometimes, positions aren't publicly advertised. Don't hesitate to reach out to companies directly with a well-crafted cover letter and resume.

Job Search on Social Media

1. LinkedIn: Optimize your LinkedIn profile to showcase your skills, experience, and career interests. Follow companies and join industry groups to stay informed about job openings.

2. Twitter and Facebook: Some companies post job openings on their Twitter or Facebook pages. Follow organizations you're interested in to receive updates.

3. Online Forums and Communities: Participate in online forums and communities related to your field. You might discover job opportunities shared by industry professionals.

Researching Companies

1. Company Research: Investigate potential employers to understand their values, culture, and mission. This information can help you tailor your applications and interview responses.

2. Industry Trends: Stay informed about trends and developments in your chosen industry. This knowledge can make you a more attractive candidate.

Tailoring Your Applications

1. Customized Resumes and Cover Letters: Customize your resume and

CHAPTER 6: JOB SEARCH STRATEGIES

cover letter for each application. Highlight relevant skills and experiences that match the job requirements.

2. Keywords: Identify keywords and phrases in job descriptions and incorporate them into your application materials. This can improve your chances of passing through applicant tracking systems.

Preparing for Interviews

1. Practice: Practice your interview skills by conducting mock interviews with career advisors, professors, or peers. Prepare answers to common interview questions.

2. Behavioral Interviews: Be ready to discuss specific situations where you demonstrated skills like teamwork, problem-solving, and leadership.

3. Research the Company: Study the organization, its culture, and the role you're applying for. Show that you're genuinely interested in the company.

Job Offer Evaluation and Negotiation

1. Evaluating Offers: Carefully assess job offers, considering factors like salary, benefits, work-life balance, and opportunities for growth.

2. Negotiation: Don't be afraid to negotiate the terms of your job offer. Research typical salary ranges for your position and be prepared to articulate your value.

Handling Rejections

1. Learn from Rejections: Use rejection as an opportunity to learn and improve. Seek feedback from interviewers, if possible.

2. Persist and Stay Positive: Job hunting can be challenging, and rejections are part of the process. Stay persistent and maintain a positive attitude.

Your job search is a dynamic process that involves research, preparation, and persistence. By utilizing diverse job search strategies, tailoring your applications, and effectively preparing for interviews, you can increase your chances of finding the right job as you prepare to enter the labor market during your final year in college or university.

Chapter 7: Interview Preparation

Job interviews are a critical phase in your transition from college or university to the labor market. This chapter delves into the strategies and tips you need to prepare effectively for interviews, whether they are in person, virtual, or conducted via phone.

The Significance of Interview Preparation

1. First Impressions: Interviews provide the opportunity to make a strong first impression on potential employers.

2. Showcasing Skills: Interviews allow you to demonstrate your skills, qualifications, and enthusiasm for the role.

3. Cultural Fit: Employers use interviews to gauge how well you might fit into their organization's culture.

Interview Preparation Essentials

1. Research the Company: Understand the organization's values, culture, products or services, recent news, and industry position. This knowledge will help you tailor your responses and ask informed questions.

2. Know the Job Description: Familiarize yourself with the job requirements and responsibilities outlined in the job posting. Be prepared to discuss how your skills and experience align with these.

3. Prepare STAR Stories: Structure your responses to behavioral questions using the STAR method (Situation, Task, Action, Result). Provide specific examples from your experiences.

Common Interview Questions

1. Tell Me About Yourself: Craft a concise, compelling response that highlights your relevant experiences and skills. Focus on what makes you a suitable candidate.

2. Strengths and Weaknesses: Discuss your strengths, focusing on those relevant to the job. When discussing weaknesses, show self-awareness and explain how you're working to improve.

3. Why Do You Want This Job?: Explain why you're interested in the role and how it aligns with your career goals and values.

4. Behavioral Questions: Be prepared to discuss situations where you demonstrated skills like teamwork, problem-solving, leadership, and adaptability.

5. Questions for the Interviewer: Prepare thoughtful questions to ask the interviewer. This demonstrates your genuine interest in the role and organization.

Virtual and Phone Interviews

1. Test Technology: Ensure your computer, camera, microphone, and internet connection are reliable. Familiarize yourself with the video conferencing platform you'll be using.

CHAPTER 7: INTERVIEW PREPARATION

2. Select a Suitable Environment: Choose a quiet, well-lit space for virtual interviews. Remove distractions and ensure your background is professional.

3. Dress Professionally: Dress as you would for an in-person interview. Professional attire can boost your confidence.

Mock Interviews

1. Practice with Peers: Conduct mock interviews with friends or peers to get comfortable answering questions and receiving feedback.

2. Career Services: Many universities offer mock interview services where professionals or career advisors simulate real interview scenarios.

On the Day of the Interview

1. Arrive Early: If the interview is in person, plan to arrive early. For virtual or phone interviews, log in or call in ahead of time to ensure you're ready when the interview begins.

2. Bring Necessary Documents: If required, bring extra copies of your resume and references. Have a notepad and pen for taking notes.

3. Body Language: Maintain good eye contact, sit up straight, and use open body language to convey confidence.

Follow-Up

1. Send a Thank-You Email: Within 24 hours of the interview, send a thank-you email to express your appreciation for the opportunity and reiterate your interest in the role.

2. Follow-Up on Promised Actions: If you agreed to provide additional

information or samples of your work, ensure you do so promptly.

Interview preparation is a key component of a successful job search. By researching the company, preparing responses to common questions, practicing with mock interviews, and presenting yourself professionally, you'll increase your chances of making a favorable impression on potential employers and securing the job you desire.

8

Chapter 8: Professional Development

As you prepare to enter the labor market during your last year in college or university, focusing on your professional development can significantly enhance your readiness and appeal to potential employers. This chapter explores the importance of honing your soft skills and participating in workshops and seminars to become a well-rounded professional.

The Significance of Professional Development

1. Continuous Improvement: Professional development fosters a growth mindset, emphasizing the importance of ongoing learning and skill enhancement.

2. Adaptability: In today's rapidly changing job market, professionals who can adapt and learn new skills are highly valued.

3. Enhanced Soft Skills: Developing soft skills like communication, teamwork, adaptability, and problem-solving can make you a more attractive candidate.

Soft Skills Development

1. Communication Skills: Effective communication, both verbal and written, is a core competency. Consider courses or workshops in public speaking, business writing, or interpersonal communication.

2. Teamwork and Collaboration: Participate in group projects, extracurricular activities, or workshops that emphasize teamwork. Learn to work harmoniously with diverse teams.

3. Adaptability: Embrace change and seek experiences that challenge you to adapt. This might include taking on leadership roles or volunteering for projects outside your comfort zone.

4. Problem-Solving and Critical Thinking: Courses in critical thinking or analytical skills can help you become a better problem solver.

Workshops and Seminars

1. University Workshops: Many universities offer workshops on various professional development topics, from resume building to interview skills. Attend these sessions to gain valuable insights.

2. Online Learning: Explore online platforms like Coursera, edX, or LinkedIn Learning for courses on leadership, time management, or other relevant skills.

3. Professional Associations: Consider joining a professional association related to your field. These organizations often host workshops and conferences that provide opportunities for skill development and networking.

Internships and Part-Time Jobs

1. Learning on the Job: Treat internships and part-time jobs as opportunities to develop practical skills. Seek feedback and use these experiences as learning opportunities.

2. Networking: Interacting with colleagues, supervisors, and mentors in the workplace can enhance your interpersonal and communication skills.

Leadership and Extracurricular Activities

1. Leadership Roles: Take on leadership positions in clubs, organizations, or volunteer activities. These roles require you to develop skills in decision-making, conflict resolution, and team management.

2. Volunteer Work: Engage in volunteer work that allows you to make a positive impact on your community while building skills like empathy and adaptability.

Mentorship and Guidance

1. Mentorship: Seek out mentors in your field who can offer guidance and provide a valuable perspective on your professional development.

2. Career Advisors: Utilize the resources at your university's career center. Career advisors can help you identify areas for development and connect you with relevant workshops or resources.

Professional Development Plans

1. Set Goals: Develop a professional development plan with clear, achievable goals for skill enhancement.

2. Track Progress: Monitor your progress, update your goals, and adjust your plan as needed to ensure continuous development.

3. Feedback: Seek feedback from mentors, professors, and peers to assess your progress and areas for improvement.

Professional development is a lifelong journey that doesn't end with graduation. By focusing on soft skills, attending workshops and seminars, and actively participating in extracurricular activities and internships, you'll not only become a more well-rounded professional but also enhance your readiness to enter the labor market with confidence and competence.

9

Chapter 9: Career Counseling

During your last year in college or university, seeking career counseling can be an invaluable resource for shaping your career path and making informed decisions. This chapter explores the benefits of career counseling and how to best leverage this guidance to tailor your career.

The Role of Career Counseling

1. Guidance and Support: Career counselors provide guidance and support in making career-related decisions, from choosing the right job to setting long-term goals.

2. Skills Assessment: Counselors help you identify your strengths, skills, and areas for improvement. They often use assessments to gain insights into your personality and preferences.

3. Exploration: Counselors assist you in exploring different career options, industries, and opportunities, helping you align your choices with your values and goals.

When to Seek Career Counseling

1. Early Planning: It's beneficial to start career counseling early in your academic journey, but the last year is an excellent time to refine your strategy.

2. Uncertainty: If you're uncertain about your career direction, or if you're considering a major change, career counseling can provide clarity.

3. Transition to the Workforce: If you're preparing to enter the labor market, career counselors can help you with job search strategies and interview preparation.

Services Offered by Career Counselors

1. Self-Assessment: Counselors use tools and discussions to help you identify your skills, interests, and values, leading to a clearer sense of your ideal career path.

2. Resume and Cover Letter Review: They can help you craft effective application materials tailored to your chosen field.

3. Interview Preparation: Counselors often conduct mock interviews to prepare you for real interviews and provide feedback.

4. Job Search Strategies: Career counselors can offer guidance on effective job search techniques and how to navigate online job boards and career fairs.

5. Career Planning: They assist in setting specific, achievable career goals and creating a plan to reach them.

6. Networking: Counselors can advise on building and leveraging your professional network.

Preparing for Career Counseling

CHAPTER 9: CAREER COUNSELING

1. Self-Reflection: Take some time to reflect on your goals, values, and areas where you might need guidance.

2. Questions: Prepare a list of questions and topics you'd like to discuss with the counselor, such as exploring specific career paths, improving your resume, or building your network.

3. Goals: Clearly define what you hope to achieve through career counseling so that you can communicate this to your counselor.

Building a Relationship with Your Counselor

1. Open Communication: Be open and honest in your discussions with the counselor. This fosters trust and helps them provide tailored advice.

2. Active Participation: Engage actively in the process, including completing assessments and following through with recommended actions.

3. Feedback: Provide feedback on the effectiveness of the counseling sessions, as this helps improve the services provided.

Leveraging University Resources

1. University Career Center: Your university's career center likely offers career counseling services. Reach out to schedule an appointment.

2. Workshops and Events: Participate in career-related workshops and events hosted by your university to gain additional insights and support.

Seeking External Career Counseling

If you feel that your university's resources aren't meeting your needs, you can consider seeking external career counseling services. These can be found through career consulting firms or individual career coaches.

Career counseling is a resource that can empower you to make informed career decisions and navigate the transition from college or university to the labor market more effectively. By actively participating in the process, you can gain valuable insights and guidance for shaping your career.

10

Chapter 10: Building a Personal Brand

In today's competitive job market, establishing a strong personal brand is essential for making a lasting impression on potential employers. This chapter explores the concept of personal branding and how you can effectively manage your online presence to enhance your career prospects.

What Is Personal Branding?

1. Your Unique Identity: Your personal brand is a combination of your skills, experiences, values, and reputation that sets you apart from others in your field.

2. Perception: It's how you're perceived by peers, colleagues, and employers. Your personal brand influences how people think of you professionally.

3. Online and Offline: Personal branding is relevant both in your online presence (e.g., social media and professional profiles) and in your day-to-day interactions.

Why Personal Branding Matters

1. Professional Opportunities: A strong personal brand can open doors to

job opportunities, partnerships, and collaborations.

2. Credibility: A well-crafted personal brand can establish you as an expert or authority in your field, enhancing your credibility.

3. Networking: A strong personal brand can attract like-minded professionals and expand your professional network.

Managing Your Online Presence

1. Consistency: Maintain a consistent image and message across all online platforms, including social media, LinkedIn, personal websites, and blogs.

2. LinkedIn Profile: Ensure your LinkedIn profile is complete, professional, and reflects your skills and accomplishments. Engage in networking and discussions on the platform.

3. Social Media Audit: Regularly review your social media posts to ensure they align with your professional image. Remove or modify content that may be detrimental.

Creating Valuable Content

1. Content Creation: Share your knowledge and insights by creating and sharing relevant content, such as articles, blog posts, videos, or presentations.

2. Thought Leadership: Position yourself as a thought leader by contributing original ideas and perspectives in your field.

3. Engagement: Interact with your online community by responding to comments, participating in discussions, and offering valuable insights.

Showcasing Your Expertise

CHAPTER 10: BUILDING A PERSONAL BRAND

1. Public Speaking: Participate in webinars, conferences, or podcasts to share your expertise.

2. Guest Posts: Write guest articles for industry publications or blogs to reach a wider audience.

3. Networking Events: Attend industry-specific events, workshops, and seminars to showcase your knowledge and build relationships.

Building a Personal Website or Blog

1. Online Portfolio: Create a personal website or blog to showcase your accomplishments, projects, and expertise.

2. Content Sharing: Regularly update your website with new content to demonstrate your commitment to your field.

Seek Feedback and Adapt

1. Feedback Loop: Request feedback from peers, mentors, and colleagues about your personal brand. Use their input to adapt and improve.

2. Continuous Learning: Stay informed about industry trends and changes, and be ready to adjust your personal brand strategy accordingly.

Monitoring Your Online Presence

1. Online Tools: Use online reputation management tools to track mentions of your name and respond to comments or reviews professionally.

2. Google Yourself: Regularly search for your name on search engines to see what comes up. Make sure the results align with your personal brand.

Personal branding is a dynamic process that requires consistent effort and adaptation. By managing your online presence, sharing valuable content, showcasing your expertise, and seeking feedback, you can establish a strong personal brand that enhances your career prospects and opens doors to professional opportunities.

11

Chapter 11: Transitioning from Academia to the Workforce

The transition from college or university to the workforce is a significant step in your life. This chapter explores the essential aspects of this transition, from managing your expectations to adjusting to a professional environment.

Managing Expectations

1. Realistic Expectations: Understand that the professional world may differ from the academic one. You may not immediately have a job that aligns perfectly with your major.

2. Learning Curve: Be prepared to learn and adapt in your new job. The skills you developed in school are valuable, but practical experience is essential.

3. Growth Takes Time: It's normal to start with an entry-level position. Your career will progress as you gain experience and expertise.

Adapting to the Workplace

1. Professional Behavior: Embrace professionalism in your interactions with colleagues and superiors. Punctuality, respect, and effective communication are crucial.

2. Office Etiquette: Familiarize yourself with office etiquette, such as dress code, email communication, and workplace norms.

3. Listening and Learning: In the early days, focus on listening, learning, and understanding your role and the company culture.

Balancing Work and Life

1. Work-Life Balance: Prioritize a healthy work-life balance. Don't overcommit or overwork yourself.

2. Time Management: Efficiently manage your time to fulfill both work responsibilities and personal life obligations.

3. Stress Management: Develop stress-coping strategies to maintain your well-being.

Networking and Building Relationships

1. Professional Networking: Continue to nurture your professional network. It's a valuable asset for your career progression.

2. Colleague Relationships: Build positive relationships with your colleagues. These connections can enhance your job satisfaction and career growth.

3. Mentorship: Seek mentors within your workplace who can provide guidance and support as you adjust to your new role.

Setting Career Goals

CHAPTER 11: TRANSITIONING FROM ACADEMIA TO THE WORKFORCE

1. Short-Term Goals: Define achievable short-term career goals. These can keep you motivated and provide direction.

2. Long-Term Aspirations: Consider your long-term career aspirations. What path do you want to follow? What skills and experiences are necessary to reach your goals?

3. Skill Development: Continuously work on developing skills that align with your career goals. Seek opportunities within your current job to gain these skills.

Staying Current

1. Industry Updates: Stay informed about industry trends and changes. Attend seminars, webinars, and workshops to keep your knowledge up to date.

2. Continuous Learning: Explore opportunities for further education, such as certifications or additional courses that can enhance your career.

3. Adaptability: Be open to adapting and evolving as the job market changes. Flexibility is a valuable skill.

Managing Finances

1. Budgeting: Create a budget to manage your finances, including expenses, savings, and investments.

2. Financial Literacy: Improve your financial literacy to make informed decisions about investments, retirement planning, and debt management.

3. Salary Negotiation: Learn to negotiate your salary and benefits to ensure you're fairly compensated.

Career Advancement

1. Proactive Approach: Don't wait for opportunities to come to you. Seek out chances for advancement, express your interest, and ask for new responsibilities.

2. Performance Evaluation: Regularly assess your performance and seek feedback from supervisors to identify areas for improvement.

3. Professional Development: Continue investing in professional development and acquiring new skills that are relevant to your career growth.

The transition from academia to the workforce is a significant life change. By managing your expectations, adapting to the professional environment, setting clear career goals, and staying current with industry trends, you can navigate this transition effectively and build a successful and satisfying career.

12

Chapter 12: Thriving in Your New Career

Congratulations, you've successfully transitioned from academia to the workforce! This final chapter explores how to not only survive but thrive in your new career. It offers guidance on long-term career development, maintaining work-life balance, and achieving professional fulfillment.

Setting Long-Term Career Goals

1. Reflection: Periodically revisit your long-term career goals. Are they still aligned with your aspirations and interests?

2. Progress Monitoring: Regularly assess your progress toward your career goals. Identify achievements and areas for improvement.

3. Skill Enhancement: Continue developing your skills and expertise in your chosen field. Seek opportunities for professional growth.

Networking and Relationship Building

1. Sustain Your Network: Maintain and expand your professional network. Networking remains vital for career progression and learning about new

opportunities.

2. Mentorship: Consider transitioning from being mentored to becoming a mentor. Sharing your knowledge can be personally fulfilling and professionally rewarding.

Work-Life Balance

1. Reassess Regularly: Balance between work and personal life can shift. Reassess your priorities periodically and make adjustments as needed.

2. Boundaries: Set clear boundaries to prevent overwork and burnout. Unplug from work when it's time to focus on personal life.

3. Self-Care: Prioritize self-care to maintain your physical and mental well-being. Regular exercise, healthy eating, and relaxation are essential.

Career Fulfillment

1. Passion and Purpose: Seek out roles and projects that align with your passions and personal values. Finding meaning in your work can lead to lasting job satisfaction.

2. Recognition and Growth: Pursue recognition for your contributions and seek opportunities for career advancement. Don't hesitate to ask for the responsibilities and opportunities that align with your career goals.

3. Professional Development: Continue to invest in professional development. Attend conferences, workshops, and courses to stay up to date with industry trends.

Financial Health

CHAPTER 12: THRIVING IN YOUR NEW CAREER

1. Savings and Investments: Continue to manage your finances wisely, emphasizing savings and investments for your future security.

2. Retirement Planning: Plan for your retirement early. Contributions to retirement accounts can compound over time.

3. Salary Negotiation: Don't stop negotiating your salary. As you gain experience and accomplishments, your market value can increase.

Work-Life Integration

1. Flexible Work Arrangements: Explore flexible work arrangements that allow you to integrate work and personal life more effectively.

2. Telecommuting and Remote Work: Depending on your field, consider opportunities for remote work that may offer a better work-life balance.

3. Quality Over Quantity: Measure your career success in terms of the quality of life and job satisfaction rather than just salary or titles.

Giving Back

1. Community Involvement: Get involved in community service or volunteer work. Giving back can be personally rewarding and enhance your professional growth.

2. Mentorship: Continue mentoring others, especially recent graduates. Sharing your experiences and insights can be a fulfilling way to contribute to the next generation.

Embracing Change

1. Adaptability: Embrace change and be open to exploring new opportunities,

even if they take you in unexpected directions.

2. Lifelong Learning: Maintain a commitment to lifelong learning. The workforce continually evolves, and staying informed is essential.

3. Resilience: Build resilience to handle challenges and setbacks in your career. Learn from failures and use them as stepping stones to future success.

Your journey from academia to the workforce is a significant achievement. By setting long-term career goals, sustaining your network, managing work-life balance, seeking career fulfillment, maintaining financial health, and giving back to your community, you can thrive in your career and create a fulfilling and prosperous professional life.

www.ingramcontent.com/pod-product-compliance
Lightning Source LLC
Chambersburg PA
CBHW070441010526
44118CB00014B/2145